USING NON-FICTION

KEY STAGE 2: Y5–6/ P6–7

FRANCES MACKAY

HOPSCOTCH

EDUCATIONAL PUBLISHING

Contents

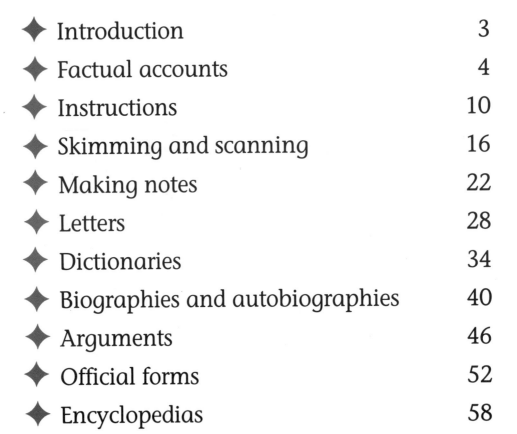

◆ Introduction   3

◆ Factual accounts   4

◆ Instructions   10

◆ Skimming and scanning   16

◆ Making notes   22

◆ Letters   28

◆ Dictionaries   34

◆ Biographies and autobiographies   40

◆ Arguments   46

◆ Official forms   52

◆ Encyclopedias   58

Published by Hopscotch Educational Publishing Company Ltd, 29 Waterloo Place, Leamington Spa CV32 5LA 01926 744227

© 1998 Hopscotch Educational Publishing

Written by Frances Mackay
Series design by Blade Communications
Illustrated by Rodney Sutton
Cover illustration by Susan Hutchison
Printed by Clintplan, Southam

Frances Mackay hereby asserts her moral right to be identified as the author of this work in accordance with the Copyright, Designs and Patents Act, 1988.

ISBN 1-902239-05-9

Introduction

ABOUT THE SERIES

Developing Literacy Skills is a series of books aimed at developing key literacy skills using stories, non-fiction, poetry and rhyme, spelling and grammar, from Key Stage 1 (P1–3) through to Key Stage 2 (P4–7).

The series offers a structured approach which provides detailed lesson plans to teach specific literacy skills. A unique feature of the series is the provision of differentiated photocopiable activities aimed at considerably reducing teacher preparation time. Suggestions for using the photocopiable pages as a stimulus for further work in the classroom is provided to ensure maximum use of this resource.

ABOUT THIS BOOK

This book is for teachers of children at Key Stage 2 Y5–6 and Scottish levels P6–7. It aims to:

✦ develop children's literacy skills through exposure to and experience of a wide range of stimulating non-fiction texts with supporting differentiated activities which are both diversified and challenging;
✦ support teachers by providing practical teaching methods based on whole-class, group, paired and individual teaching;
✦ encourage enjoyment and curiosity as well as develop skills of interpretation and response.

CHAPTER CONTENT

Overall aims

These outline the aims for both lessons set out in each chapter.

Suggested books/texts

This lists the types of books/texts that could be used in the lessons to support the literacy skill being addressed in the lesson.

Intended learning

This sets out the specific aims for each individual lesson within the chapter.

Starting point

This provides ideas for introducing the activity and may include key questions to ask the children.

Activity

This explains the task(s) the children will carry out in the lesson without supporting photocopiable activities.

Using the differentiated activity sheets

This explains how to use each sheet as well as providing guidance on the type of child who will benefit most from each sheet.

Plenary session

This suggests ideas for whole-class sessions to discuss the learning outcomes and follow-up work.

Using the photocopiable sheets as a stimulus for further work

This is a useful list of further activities that can be developed from the activity sheets. These ideas maximise the use of the photocopiable pages.

Other ideas for using . . .

This contains other ideas for developing the skills explored in each chapter. The ideas will have completely different learning intentions from the featured lessons and provide a range of alternatives.

And finally . . .

Page 64 contains a generic photocopiable activity sheet for children to use to evaluate different non-fiction texts.

Overall aims

✦ To compare features of factual writing, such as accounts of visits and events, anecdotes, diaries, observational writing and reports.
✦ To draft, edit and refine a factual account about a school visit.

 ## Suggested text

A copy of the text below for each child.

 ### LESSON ONE

 ## Intended learning

✦ To compare the features and purposes of different types of factual accounts.

 ## Starting point: Whole class

✦ Share the text with the class. Can the children decide which piece of writing is a police report, a diary extract, news report or an eye-witness account? What do they base their decisions on?
✦ Compare the degrees of formality used in the language of the accounts. Why would a police report need to be more formal, for example?

 ✦ What other information would help the accounts? Would a picture of the car or a photofit of the thief be useful? Is chronological order of events important? For which account?

 ## Group activities

✦ Working in groups of four, the children should invent a story where a crime has taken place. Tell them to talk through their ideas and agree on all the facts. Give a time limit – say five to 10 minutes.
✦ Next ask either each member of the group or the whole group together to write four paragraphs giving an account of the crime in the same way as those presented below. Encourage them to help each other so that the group as a whole contributes to each account.

Plenary session

Bring the whole class together again. Ask one person from a group to tell the story of their crime. Then ask the other members to read out their accounts. How well does the oral account match up with the written ones? How well do the four accounts match up? Do they contradict or complement each other? Is the language appropriate? Is the purpose of the account clear? Which account was the easiest to write? Why? How could they be improved?

First of all I saw a man looking into the car then he walked away. Five minutes later, he was back. He had something in his hand but I couldn't see what it was. Before I could do anything, he got into the car and drove off. I couldn't stop him, so I rang the police.

Thursday 10th November, 3.40pm. Red Ferrari stolen from outside Hilton Hotel. Estimated time of theft 3.15pm. Mr Ted Blake, the only witness, claims he saw a man aged about 20 years, wearing blue jeans and a red shirt, steal the car. The car is owned by a Miss Rachael Headington.

Today at 3.15pm a man described as 20 years old and wearing blue jeans and a red shirt, stole a valuable Ferrari from outside the Hilton Hotel. A witness said the man had the car unlocked and started up within seconds. A large reward is offered for any information leading to the recovery of the vehicle.

Today my beautiful red Ferrari was stolen. I'm so angry! I only left the car for a little while and now it's gone. Dad will go mad because he warned me not to take it. I hope he's in a good mood tomorrow!

 Developing literacy Skills

◆ LESSON TWO ◆

◆ Intended learning

◆ To draft, edit and refine a factual account about a school visit.

◆ Starting point: Whole class

◆ Ask the children to remind you of the tasks carried out in Lesson 1. What kind of writing was it? How does it differ from story writing?

◆ Tell the children they are going to try some report writing today about a school visit. Ask them to recall a recent class visit or school event. Write up a list of the main facts about this event - such as day, date, place, time the event started, what happened in order, who was there, what time the event finished and so on.

◆ Model writing a report for the children. Explain how to use the notes to form sentences about the event. Remind them about the importance of sequencing the facts in the correct order. Which is the most important information? Can anything be left out? Discuss how to write the information in the past tense, indicating verb changes. Will the report be written in the first or third person? How does this affect the writing?

◆ Go through the editing process with the children. Model reading through the report, checking the notes to make sure all the information is given. Can the wording be improved in any way to make the report sound better? Discuss punctuation and spelling and remind them about using a dictionary or thesaurus to help them. Make changes to the report until everyone is happy about the final piece. Explain that they will now carry out a similar task using an activity sheet.

◆ Using the differentiated activity sheets

Activity sheet 1

This is aimed at those children who need support in writing a report. It is a cloze activity where they are required to use the notes to complete the report. Some capital letters and full stops have been omitted.

Activity sheet 2

This is aimed at more independent writers who are capable of writing their own report from the notes provided.

Activity sheet 3

This is aimed at more able children. It requires them to sort through the information given and decide on the most relevant facts to include in the report.

◆ Plenary session

Bring the whole class together again to share the children's work. Ask someone who completed Activity sheet 1 to read out their report. Do the others in this group agree with the answers? Ask all the children in the class to agree where the capital letters and full stops should go in this report. Ask some children from the other groups to read out their reports. Do the others agree they sound like good accounts? Have they described the events well? Are the reports written in the past tense? Is all the information relevant?

Discuss the task itself. What difficulties were encountered? How were these overcome?

Factual accounts

USING THE PHOTOCOPIABLE SHEETS AS A STIMULUS FOR FURTHER WORK

✦ Make a class book about whole-school events and outings. Ask the children to be reporters for each class in the school, take notes about events and outings and then write up the reports. Ask the children to read their finished reports to the other classes. Are the facts correct? Has anything important been left out? Edit reports if necessary and then write up final copies. Put the finished book into the school library where all classes can share the reports. Make it an annual event!

✦ Find out about the places mentioned on the activity sheets. Use information books and tourist brochures to find the information and write a factual account about the places.

✦ Ask the children to imagine they were actually part of the visit to the places on the activity sheets. Ask them to write a diary account about the outing, stressing their personal feelings.

✦ Ask the children to imagine that something terrible or strange happened on the school visit. Write news reports for television or radio about the event. Ask the children to act out the reports.

✦ Visit the places mentioned in the activity sheets and write 'real' reports about them!

✦ Send for brochures about each of the places mentioned in the activity sheets. Ask each child to draw something that can be found at each site and write a brief description of it. Mix up the pictures and labels. Can the children match the writing to the correct picture?

✦ After research, ask the children to write an historical account of something that happened at one of the sites mentioned.

OTHER IDEAS FOR USING FACTUAL ACCOUNTS

✦ Write a school newspaper. Interview teachers, children and school staff. Write about school events and outings. Have a classified section and advertise forthcoming events. Use IT to create a professional paper.

✦ Spend time modelling how to write science reports and observations to give the children confidence when tackling the task in future.

✦ Ask the children to write a brief account of particular lessons during the week. At the beginning of the following week, share the accounts. Use this time to review the lessons and to make notes of any problems or difficulties the children encountered.

✦ Have a class journal where the teacher writes to the children and the children have an opportunity to write back.

✦ Encourage the children to write subject journals where they can write personal thoughts about the lessons and activities experienced. Conference with the children occasionally to share these journals.

✦ Use prepared writing frames to help the children learn how to write factual accounts for different subject areas.

◆ A school visit ◆

✦ Use these notes about a school visit to complete the report below.
　Decide where the capital letters and full stops should be.

- Thursday 11th June
- coach arrives at school at 8.45am
- Mr Tucker leads Year 5 to coach
- coach leaves school at 9.00am
- arrive at Roman Baths in Bath at 10.00am
- meet Mrs Young, the guide
- tour Baths, Jamal nearly falls in
- look at Roman things on display
- visit the gift shop
- lunch at 12.30pm
- shopping in Bath 1.00–1.30pm
- arrive back at school 3.00pm

On Thursday 11th _____ Year 5 went on a class visit to the _____

in Bath. The coach arrived at school at _____ and Mr _____ took Year 5 out

to the coach. The _____ at 9.00am. When

they arrived at the _____ in _____ they were met by

_____ who was _____. They then went on a

tour of _____ and during the tour Jamal _____.

Mr Tucker and _____ looked at _____

and then they _____. They had

_____ at 12.30pm and then they _____.

The class arrived back at school at _____

✦ Read through your report. Check with the notes to make sure you have written the
　correct things in the spaces. Make sure you have included all the capital letters and
　full stops. Check your spellings carefully.

◆ A school visit ◆

◆ Use these notes about a school visit to write a report. Decide on the correct
order of the events. Write your report in sentences.

- Monday 18th May
- arrive Caerphilly Castle, Glamorgan, Wales, 10.00 am
- Rush Grove County Primary
- tour castle, the largest in Wales
- Mrs Ford, Year 5
- complete quiz sheet about castle
- coach arrives at school 8.45am
- lunch at 12.00
- Mrs Ford counts 32 children onto coach
- draw Leaning Tower and gatehouses
- coach leaves at 9.00am
- arrive back at school 3.00pm

◆ Write your report in the space below. Use a dictionary to help you.

◆ Read through your report. Does it make sense? Have you included all the information?
Are the events in the right order? Use a red pen to change anything to improve the
report. Check the punctuation and spelling.

Developing
literacy
Skills

◆ A school visit ◆

◆ Read these notes about a school visit. Underline the information you think should be included in a report about the visit. Use this information to write a report. Write in sentences.

- Friday 2nd October
- mild, sunny day with slight breeze
- Rush Grove County Primary
- Year 5 class, 30 children
- class teacher, Miss Kinnear
- adult helpers, Mr Singh and Mrs Maggs
- Hilltop Coaches
- coach arrives at school 8.45am
- coach leaves school at 9.00am
- all people are wearing seat belts
- coach travels at 35mph

- lovely scenery on the way
- Scott feels sick on coach
- Samantha loses her pencil behind the seat
- arrive Avebury 10.30am
- eat morning snack, Jane breaks her ruler
- walk around stone circle, Tom falls over
- draw several stones using charcoal
- visit Folk Life Museum, buy souvenir
- eat lunch at 1pm near Old Barn
- do activity sheet at Alexander Keiller Museum
- arrive back at school 3.00pm

◆ Read through your report. Have you included all the relevant information? Are the events in the correct order? Use a red pen to change anything to improve the report.

◆ Check your punctuation. Use a dictionary to check your speliings.

Instructions

 Overall aims

✦ To discuss the organisation and layout of different types of instructions.
✦ To write own instructions.

 Suggested texts

A collection of examples of different kinds of instructions, such as sheets that are provided with self-assembly furniture or construction kit model-making, books on making toys, manuals on how to set up equipment such as a television or computer and so on.

 **LESSON ONE**

 Intended learning

✦ To discuss the organisation and layout of instructional texts.
✦ To make an agreed list of the features of 'good' instructions.

 Starting point: Whole class

✦ Ask the children to tell you when they last used a set of instructions. What were the instructions used for? Write a list of all the things the children can think of where instructions are needed.
✦ How important is it to have instructions? Do people always use the instructions provided with new equipment, for example? Why or why not? Go through the list and agree on those where it would be absolutely vital to follow the exact instructions and those where it would not.
✦ Ask the children to tell you the difficulties they or their parents have encountered when using instructions. Consider computer game instructions, for example, are they always easy to follow?
✦ Write up a class list of the things the children think are important in instructions. What makes a 'good' set of instructions?

 ✦ Tell them that they are going to consider this further by looking at a collection of instructions.

 Group activities

✦ Provide each group with a copy of the same four or five instructions taken from various sources. Include in the collection a very difficult and hard-to-follow instruction page as well as a very easy-to-use and clear text.
✦ Ask each group to read through the texts and do the following tasks:
a) Rank the texts in order from the most difficult to the easiest to read and understand.
b) Write a couple of sentences about the top and bottom ranked texts – why they are difficult/easy.
c) Write down two ideas on how to improve each set of instructions.
✦ Encourage the children to work collaboratively and to come to a group agreement for each task if possible.

Plenary session

Bring the whole class together again when the tasks have been completed to share their responses. Compare the ranking of the texts – is there any agreement? What makes the top ranked text so difficult to read and understand? How could it be improved? Why is the bottom ranked text so easy to use? Share the ideas about improving the instructions. Discuss layout – how numbering, bullet points and/or diagrams help. Are headings helpful? Is it easier to read if the text is set out in clear divisions or paragraphs? Refer back to the agreed list of what makes a 'good' set of instructions. Add new ideas in the light of the plenary discussion. Display this list after the lesson so the children can refer to it.

LESSON TWO

Intended learning

+ To discuss the organisation and layout of instructions for making things.
+ To write own instructions.

Starting point: Whole class

+ Provide the children with a copy of the same instructions for making something (from a craft book, for example).
+ Ask the children to follow the instructions as you read them out. Discuss the general layout of the page. How is it set out? Are there separate headings to make things easier to find? Is the introduction clear? How are the materials needed set out? What method is used to set out the steps involved – numbers, paragraphs, bullet points? Are the diagrams clear and well labelled?
+ How is the information written? Is it in note form or full sentences? Are there any technical terms used? Does everything appear to be sequential?
+ How does this set of instructions compare with the list of features 'good' instructions should have which was compiled in Lesson 1? How could these instructions be improved?
+ Tell the children they will now have the opportunity to write their own set of instructions, keeping this list of features in mind.

Using the differentiated activity sheets

Activity sheet 1

This activity is designed for those children who need support in writing their own instructions. The activity is presented as a cloze sheet, where the children have to use the diagrams to help them decide on the best word to use to complete the instructions.

Activity sheet 2

This activity is for those children who are more independent writers as they are required to write the instructions to match a set of diagrams.

Activity sheet 3

This activity is for more able children. They are required to make a 'mock-up' design of a pop-up card and then draw and write the instructions for making their card.

Plenary session.

After the children have completed their tasks, bring the whole class together again. Ask someone from each group to explain what they had to do, then share some examples from each group. Do the others agree their instructions are clear and well written? Has anything important been left out? How difficult was it to write the instructions? What are good points to keep in mind?

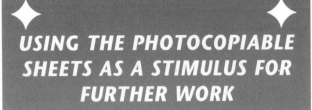

USING THE PHOTOCOPIABLE SHEETS AS A STIMULUS FOR FURTHER WORK

✦ Swap the instruction sheets with children in a different group – can they make the object using the instructions? Ask the children to pair up afterwards to discuss how successful each other's instructions were.

✦ Make a class book of things to make with the activity sheets as the first three pages. Ask the children to design and make other objects to include in the book and then write up the instructions on how to make them.

✦ Cut out the diagrams and instructions separately. Can children from another group match the instructions to the correct diagram?

✦ Simplify instructions. Ask the children to work in pairs or small groups to improve instructions in craft books. Can they turn the instructions into four simple steps and set them out as in the activity sheets?

✦ Collect other examples of instructions for making puppets, kites and cards. Make class books for the children to share.

OTHER IDEAS FOR USING INSTRUCTIONS

✦ Explore different subject content by asking the children to write instructions on how to do things specifically related to a subject, for example: how to do a maths procedure, how to start up the computer, how to create an artistic effect, how to play a particular PE game and so on.

✦ Make a useful book on life-saving skills. Ask the children to find out about road safety, first aid, stranger danger and so on. Then ask them to write some instructions on what to do in particular situations. Display the book in the school library so others can benefit from the information.

✦ Have a hunt to find the worst set of instructions ever!! Ask the children to involve adults at home as well. Bring in copies of the very worst instructions – are self-assembly ones the most difficult to follow? Write to the manufacturers with a list of faults in the instructions to hopefully improve future versions!

✦ How important is the text? Cut out the text from instructions and ask the children to make the object using the diagrams only. Is it possible? Can the children write the text? Compare it with the original.

✦ Make up fantasy instructions – How to become a millionaire, how to make your enemies disappear, how to get out of homework and so on.

✦ Make an instruction book for aliens. Ask the children to write the instructions for everyday activities so that an alien would know what to do, for example, how to make a bed, how to make an omelette, how to wash a car and so on. Ask others to check over the instructions to make sure they are clear and nothing important has been left out.

✦ Making a puppet ✦

✦ Look at the diagrams below. They show you how to make a glove puppet. Complete the instructions for each one.

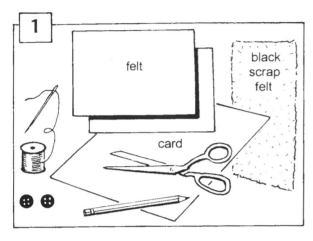

1

You will need:
2 _____ of felt (16_____ x _____)
a pair of _____
two _____
needle and _____
_____ _____ felt
a pencil and some _____

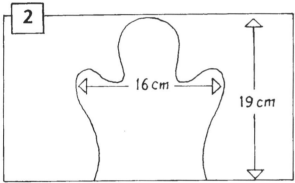

2

Draw a shape like the _____ in the diagram _____ a piece of card.
_____ around the _____ to make a template.
Use the _____ to cut out two _____ of felt.

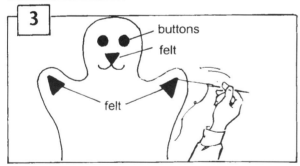

3

On one piece of _____, sew on two _____ for eyes.
Use some black scrap _____ to sew on a _____ and some paws.
Sew or draw on a _____.

4

Sew the two _____ of felt together.
Leave the straight edge _____ for your hand to go in.
Cut _____ some more scrap _____ to make some _____.
Sew on the _____.

◆ Making a kite ◆

◆ Look at the diagrams below. They show you how to make a kite.
Write the instructions for each one.

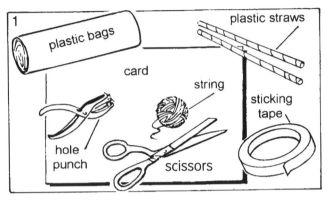
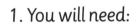

1. You will need:

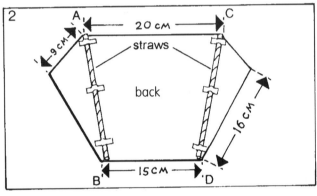

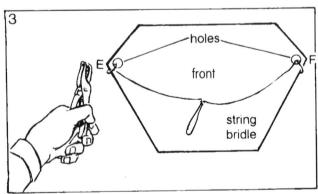

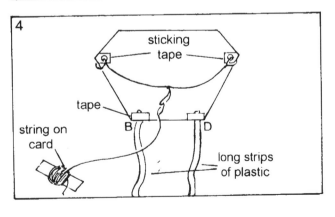

14 **Using non-fiction**
KS2: Y5–6/P6–7

Developing
Literacy
Skills

Photocopiable

©Hopscotch Educational Publishing

◆ Making a pop-up card ◆

◆ Use scrap paper to make a pop-up card of your own design. Then, in the boxes below, draw the diagrams and write the instructions for how to make it .

Diagram of items needed	Written list of items needed

Diagram of first step in making the card	Instructions to go with diagram 1

Diagram of next step	Instructions to go with diagram 2

Diagram of final step	Instructions for final diagram

Using non-fiction

Developing
literacy
Skills

Photocopiable

KS2: Y5–6/P6–7

©Hopscotch Educational Publishing

15

Overall aims

♦ To learn how to use skimming and scanning techniques to locate information quickly.
♦ To practise skimming and scanning linked to science work.

 ## Suggested texts

Dictionaries, telephone directories, newspapers and information books with contents and index pages.

 ## LESSON ONE

 ## Intended learning

♦ To learn how to use skimming and scanning techniques to locate information quickly.

 ## Starting point: Whole class

♦ Write the terms 'skimming' and 'scanning' on the board. Explain to the children that these terms refer to methods that can be used to find information quickly – skimming is usually used to find the right page or paragraph.
♦ Let the children practise skimming. Using telephone directories and/or dictionaries, show them how to use the guide words to locate the required page. Have races using copies of the same dictionary or directory to find specific guide words. Then practise skimming contents and index pages of information books to find key words.
♦ Use the same copy of a newspaper page to hunt for key words in headings. How quickly can they find a word beginning with....? Then specific words.
♦ Explain that scanning is used once the correct page or article is found. Show them how to read the first line of a paragraph or the words in bold on a page in order to obtain an idea of what the paragraph might be about. Tell them that in order to scan a page quickly, they need to omit any text they think is unlikely to contain the information they are looking for.

♦ Practise this technique by providing the children with the same copy of a page from an information book. Ask them to find the answer to a particular question. Show them how to scan through the paragraphs until they find one which is likely to contain the answer. Repeat this several times until the children understand how to go about scanning the page quickly.

 ## Group activities

♦ Ask the children to time each other skimming through dictionaries or directories to find particular guide words.
♦ How many words can they find in a newspaper page? Ask them to find a particular word or words that begin with a certain letter string.
♦ Working in pairs, ask them to devise questions for their partner to answer, using an information book. How quickly can the partner scan the page to find the answer?
♦ Make a list of companies from the Yellow Pages. Ask the children to find their telephone numbers. How quickly can they find them?
♦ Which page of an information book is most likely to have the answer to a particular question? Challenge the children to use the contents and index pages only to suggest which page the answer might be on.

Plenary session

Bring the whole class together again to share what they found out. Did they find they became quicker at skimming and scanning with practise? What tips can they share with others to make things easier? Compare answers for the company telephone numbers, newspaper words and contents/index activities. What problems did they encounter? Discuss how to overcome these. Talk about how skimming and scanning can help with school research activities.

 Developing Literacy Skills

Using non-fiction

Skimming and scanning

LESSON TWO

Intended learning

◆ To practise skimming and scanning linked to science work.

◆ Starting point: Whole class

◆ Ask the children to remind you what the terms skimming and scanning mean. Tell them that they will be practising these methods again today.
◆ Provide the children with a copy of a contents page and some paragraphs from an information book. Then ask them similar questions to those on the photocopiable activity sheets. Remind them how to use words in bold or the first lines of paragraphs to work out which paragraph might contain the information they require.
◆ Tell the children that they will now carry out the same task using an activity sheet about forces.

Using the differentiated activity sheets

All three sheets are very similar but they are differentiated by reading ability as well as scientific content.

Activity sheet 1

This activity is aimed at those children who need more support. The teacher may need to work with this group to help with the reading.

Activity sheet 2

This activity is aimed at more independent workers. Some inference is required, such as relating bridges to structures and parachutes to air resistance.

Activity sheet 3

This activity is for more able children. The scientific content is more advanced and the questions require the children to use deduction and inference.

Plenary session

Bring the whole class together again when they have completed the tasks. Compare the answers for each group's work. Ask some children from each group to say one thing they learned about forces from doing the activity. Relate the information to any relevant activities recently carried out in the classroom. Remind the children to use their skimming and scanning techniques the next time they need to find out some information.

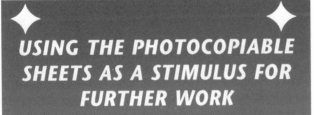

Skimming and scanning

USING THE PHOTOCOPIABLE SHEETS AS A STIMULUS FOR FURTHER WORK

✦ Make a class book about forces, beginning with the information gained from the activity sheets. Write a contents and index page for the book. Make up some question cards to go with the book to encourage the children to skim and scan.

✦ Ask each group to become 'experts', that is, Activity sheet 1 children become experts on general information about forces, Activity sheet 2 – friction and Activity sheet 3 – gravity. Ask the children to use reference books to find out more information and present a five minute talk to the rest of the class.

✦ Make a class science dictionary on forces, beginning with words on the activity sheets. Ask the children to use reference books and dictionaries to write their definitions.

✦ Display a class collection of books on forces. Make up crossword puzzles which relate to the collection to encourage use of contents page, index, headings, glossaries and so on.

✦ Use CD-ROMs to find more information relating to forces. Create a fact sheet using a desk-top publishing program.

✦ Ask the children to come up with further questions which could be asked about their activity sheets. Try out the questions on a partner.

OTHER IDEAS FOR USING SKIMMING AND SCANNING

✦ Continually model how to locate information using skimming and scanning techniques when introducing new topics in any subject area in order to reinforce **how** to find information rather than concentrating on finding the correct answer.

✦ Use part of each library session to practise locating information – perhaps have a different question each week. How quickly can the children locate the answer?

✦ Reinforce spelling activities by asking the children to skim and scan directories and newspapers to find similar sounds, rhymes or letter patterns.

✦ Read information books aloud to the children as well as story books. Model how to find sections in the book on particular topics by skimming and scanning before you read the chosen section.

✦ Ask the children to skim and scan through information books to find out how many headings, charts, diagrams or captions they can find. Compare the layout of different information books and how the organisation helps us to locate information quickly.

✦ Practise guessing what the content of a paragraph or page is by reading the first and last sentences.

◆ Forces ◆

✦   Skim through the contents page below to answer the questions.

<table>
<tr><td colspan="3">Forces by G. R. Avity</td></tr>
<tr><td colspan="3">Contents</td></tr>
<tr><td>Chapter 1</td><td>What are forces?</td><td>4</td></tr>
<tr><td>Chapter 2</td><td>Changing shapes</td><td>6</td></tr>
<tr><td>Chapter 3</td><td>Magnets</td><td>9</td></tr>
<tr><td>Chapter 4</td><td>Friction</td><td>12</td></tr>
<tr><td>Chapter 5</td><td>Gravity</td><td>16</td></tr>
<tr><td>Chapter 6</td><td>Forces and air</td><td>18</td></tr>
<tr><td>Chapter 7</td><td>Floating and sinking</td><td>20</td></tr>
</table>

In which chapter might you find information on:

magnets _____

why things float _____

how things move through the air _____

how gravity works _____

what a force is _____

what friction is _____

how shapes can change _____

why things sink _____

✦   Now, scan these paragraphs to answer the questions.

What is a force?
A force is a push or a pull. Forces can change the shape of things. Forces can make things speed up, slow down, change direction or stop.

What causes forces?
Forces can occur naturally, for example, gravity. People can make forces happen when they push or pull things such as when they use levers, pulleys or wheels.

How do forces behave?
Forces always act in pairs. For example, a toy boat sitting on water will push down on the water but the water also pushes upwards on the boat. If the forces are balanced or equal to each other, the boat will float.

Which paragraph is most likely to have the answer to these questions? Write 1, 2 or 3.

What causes forces to happen? _____
What is a force? _____
What is special about the way forces behave? _____

On the back of this sheet, write the answers to these questions:

1. What is a force?
2. Name one natural kind of force.
3. If something floats are the forces balanced or unbalanced?

◆ Forces ◆

◆ Skim through the contents page below to answer the questions.

Forces by F. R. Iction

Contents

Forces – an introduction	4
Measuring forces	5
Structures	6
Magnetism	9
Friction	12
Gravity	14
Air resistance	16
Floating and sinking	18

In which chapter might you find information on:

definition of a force _____

how magnets work _____

forces in bridges _____

how gravity works _____

how parachutes work _____

why boats float _____

how to measure forces _____

what causes forces to happen _____

◆ Now, scan these paragraphs to answer the questions.

Friction is a force. It is the force that happens when two objects rub against each other. When objects slide against each other, the friction between them causes a resistance against the movement. This causes moving objects to slow down. If the surfaces of the two objects are very smooth, there is very little friction and they slide very easily over one another. If the surfaces are rough or uneven, the friction is greater and the movement is more difficult.

Friction can be very useful. The rough surface on trainers stops you sliding on smooth surfaces. Bumpy tyres help cars to grip the road surface.

Friction can be a problem because it slows things down, wears away surfaces and produces heat. One way to reduce friction is to lubricate the surfaces. Oil is used as a lubricant in machines to stop two surfaces rubbing together.

Which paragraph is most likely to have the answers to these questions – 1, 2 or 3?

What is good about friction? _____

How does friction work? _____

What is friction? _____

What is bad about friction? _____

On the back of this sheet, write the answers to these questions:

1. Does friction speed up or slow down objects?

2. If two smooth surfaces rub against each other, will there be a lot or little friction?

3. Name one way to reduce friction.

Developing
Literacy
Skills

◆ Forces ◆

◆ Skim through the contents page below to answer the questions.

Forces by I.M. Inmotion

Contents
Understanding forces   4
Structural forces   6
Mechanical forces   8
Magnetism   10
Friction   12
Gravity   14
Air resistance   16
Floating and sinking   18

In which chapter might you find information on:

streamlining _____

definition of a force _____

magnetic induction _____

strength of buildings _____

levers and pulleys _____

buoyancy _____

how parachutes work _____

measuring forces _____

◆ Now, scan these paragraphs to answer the questions.

Gravity is a force. It is the force that pulls objects down towards the Earth. Gravity depends on the mass (the amount of matter in an object) of two objects. Earth has a large mass, so the force of attraction between an object and itself is strong so this force pulls the object towards the Earth.

Weight is a force. It is the force of gravity due to the pull of the Earth. Weight is measured in newtons. 1 kg on Earth weighs approximately 10 newtons. Because weight depends on the pull of gravity, an object would weigh less on the Moon than on Earth, even though the mass is the same. This is because the Moon is smaller than the Earth and has less mass, so the force of gravity pulling an object downwards on the Moon is smaller than on Earth. The gravity on the Moon is about one-sixth of that on Earth.

On Earth, objects of the same size, shape and material fall at the same speed, even if they do not weigh the same. Objects of the same weight but different sizes or shapes do not fall at the same speed due to air resistance. The greater the surface area of an object, the more air can get underneath the object to slow down the rate of fall. Without air, all objects would fall at the same rate.

Which paragraph is most likely to have the answers to these questions – 1, 2 or 3?

Does the Moon have gravity? _____

What do newtons measure? _____

What is air resistance? _____

What is mass? _____

What is gravity? _____

What is the difference in gravity on Earth and on the Moon? _____

On the back of this sheet, write the answers to these questions:
1. What is mass?
2. What is weight?
3. What is gravity?
4. What does air resistance do?

Making notes

 Overall aims

✦ To explore the purposes of note-making.
✦ To learn note-making techniques.
✦ To practise making notes.

 Suggested texts

Information books, newspaper classifieds, dictionaries.

 **LESSON ONE**

 Intended learning

✦ To learn different note-making techniques.
✦ To practise making notes.

 Starting point: Whole class

✦ Ask the children to give you examples of times when people take notes. Explain that at school we often need to make notes – when we are researching a topic, watching a television programme or listening to a radio programme or a visiting speaker.
✦ Explain that note-making can be quite difficult to do but they can learn special ways of doing it which will help them.
✦ **Provide a photocopy of the information about hedgehogs at the bottom of this page.** Read it with the class and ask them how they might go about writing some notes about the extract.
✦ Discuss and model the following note-making techniques using the extract:

– underlining the key words and phrases and making a list of them
– drawing and labelling a diagram of the hedgehog
– writing a table of information using these headings: body features, habitat, life cycle.

 Using the differentiated activity sheets

Activity sheet 1

This activity is aimed at less able children as the note making tasks are simple and well structured.

Activity sheet 2

This activity is for more independent workers and requires them to make a list and complete a diagram and table.

Activity sheet 3

This activity is for more able children. The text is more comprehensive and the tasks less structured. These children may need a reference book to check the accuracy of their own diagram.

 Plenary session

Share the children's responses. Ask several of them to use their notes to tell the others something about flowering plants. Will the notes and diagrams help them to remember the names of the flower parts?

The adult hedgehog is about 18–26cm in length. It has dark brown to black spines on its back and the top of the head. The rest of the body has coarse hair. It has a pointed snout, black eyes and short legs. The front feet have five digits with strong claws.

They live in dry open areas with bushes or shrubs. It is rare to find them in dense woodlands.

Hedgehogs breed from May to July and give birth in June to September. The female has two to nine young which are born blind, deaf and helpless. Their eyes open after 14 days.

The females look after the young which leave the nest after three weeks, following along behind the mother.

Making notes

Intended learning

✦ To identify different kinds of note-making and discuss their purpose.
✦ To learn how to abbreviate notes.

Starting point: Whole class

✦ Remind the children about the note-making tasks carried out in Lesson 1. Can they think of other times when people make notes? List the different kinds, such as reminder lists, planning diagrams/notes, noticeboard messages, telegrams, E-mail, memos and newspaper classified advertisements.
✦ Ask the children to tell you why they think these kinds of notes do not need to be written in sentence form. What purpose do they serve? Who will use them?
✦ How could note-making be made easier? Discuss the use of shorthand and abbreviations.
✦ Provide some classified advertisements from a newspaper. Discuss some of the abbreviations used. Why is it important to make advertisements as short as possible? What factors are involved?
✦ What other kinds of abbreviations are the children aware of? Discuss the term acronym and make a list of some of the examples children know about, such as RSPCA.
✦ Introduce the term 'mnemonics' and explain that this method can be used to help summarise information as well as remember it. Do the children know any mnemonics, such as 'Every Good Boy Deserves Fruit' which is used to remember the music notes that occur on the lines in a stave.
✦ Suggest to the children that they should try out some of these forms of abbreviation when they carry out their own note-making.

Activities

✦ Ask the children to work in pairs and use dictionaries to make a list of as many acronyms they can find.
✦ Use dictionaries to add to the class list of abbreviations.
✦ Make up some mnemonics to summarise and help memorise particular facts or information.
✦ Review classified ad sections of newspapers and make up some classified advertisements of their own to sell particular classroom objects.

Plenary session

Bring the whole class together again to share the children's work. How many acronyms and abbreviations could be found? What mnemonics were invented? Share some of the classified ads.

Review the skills learned in Lessons 1 and 2. Discuss how some of these techniques can be used when researching for school projects. Explain how helpful it is to use notes, diagrams, tables and lists instead of copying out chunks of text from books when asked to write things in 'your own words'.

Note: *I See What You Mean 1* and *I See What You Mean 2* by Alison Kilpatrick, Patricia McCall and Sue Palmer (Oliver and Boyd). These books provide excellent lesson plans for a variety of activities in note-making techniques with actual examples to use with the children.

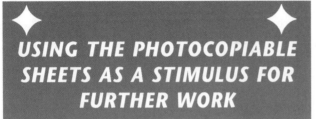

Making notes

USING THE PHOTOCOPIABLE SHEETS AS A STIMULUS FOR FURTHER WORK

✦ Ask the children to prepare a talk to the class about flowering plants, using their notes.

✦ Use the information to make a class or group book about flowering plants.

✦ Make up crossword puzzles or word searches using key words from the activity sheets.

✦ Make 3-D models of flowers. Label the parts and make an information book to go with the model.

✦ Make a flower dictionary, beginning with terms used on the sheets.

✦ Use information books to make an ABC wall mural of flowering plant words.

✦ Carry out a survey to find out the names of the children's favourite flowers.

✦ Children using Activity sheet 3 could write a list of steps involved in pollination and fertilisation.

✦ Use a desk-top publishing program to design an information sheet about flowers.

OTHER IDEAS FOR MAKING NOTES

✦ Explore ways of presenting ideas and knowledge in note form, such as concept maps, topic webs and brainstorms.

✦ Practise making sentences shorter. Delete unnecessary or repeated words in order to reduce text. Use the contracted sentences as notes.

✦ Make notes about the content of information books by writing a list of the headings and sub-headings used in the books. Display this in the reference section of the book corner so that other children can quickly find out what is in the books.

✦ Explore how explicit the children's notes are. Ask the children to use someone else's notes to write a paragraph about the topic. Were the most important/most relevant facts included in the original notes?

✦ Ask the children to write notes for a partner to use to do a drawing or diagram of an object, animal or plant. How accurate are the notes? Is it possible to do the diagram just from the notes?

✦ Use notes for specific purposes such as class debates or talks.

✦ Make up some funny acronyms!

✦ Invent some rhyming abbreviations for children's names in the class :
    'In the BC sits Miss T
    Reading Mr RD's BFG.'

◆ Flowering plants ◆

◆ You are going to make some notes about flowering plants.
Read the information below then complete the tasks.

Flowering plants have many different parts.

The <u>petals</u> are often brightly coloured to attract insects and sometimes birds.

Holding the petals together is a bowl-shaped base called a <u>receptacle</u>.

Underneath the receptacle is the <u>stem</u> which holds the plant up. The stem usually has <u>leaves</u> on it.

The <u>roots</u> are at the base of the stem.

Inside the flower itself are the reproductive parts. Most flowers have both male and female parts.

In the centre of the flower is the <u>female</u> part. It is called the pistil. At the top of the pistil is the <u>stigma</u>. Then there is a long tube called the <u>style</u>. At the base of the style is a rounded part called the <u>ovary</u>. Inside the ovary are eggs.

Surrounding the pistil are the <u>male</u> parts of the flower. They are called stamens. Each stamen has an <u>anther</u> at the top with a stem called a <u>filament</u>.

Task 1

Use the underlined words to complete these notes about flowering plants.

Flowering plants have different parts.
- the _____ attracts insects
- the _____ holds the petals
- the _____ holds the plant up and has _____ on it
- at the base of the stem are _____
- pistil – the _____ part, has a _____ , _____ and _____
- stamen – the _____ part, has an _____ and _____

Task 2

Use these notes and the information to label this diagram:

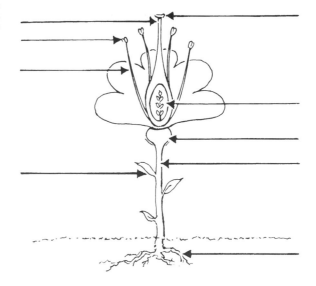

Developing
Literacy
Skills

Name _____

✦ Flowering plants ✦

✦ You are going to make some notes about flowering plants.
Read the information then complete the tasks.

Flowering plants have many special parts that are adapted for different purposes. The flowers are the reproductive part of a plant. Most flowers have both male and female parts.

The female part is called the pistil. It is usually in the centre of the flower. The pistil has several parts to it. The top is called the stigma, then there is a long tube called a style which ends in a rounded base called the ovary. Inside the ovary are many eggs.

There are usually several male parts, called stamens. They have an anther at the top and a long stem called a filament.

Petals surround the pistil and stamens. They are brightly coloured to attract insects and sometimes birds. The petals all join together at the base of the flower in an area called the receptacle. The stem holds the flower upright and usually has many leaves on it. At the base of the stem are the roots.

✦ Underline the important words and phrases in the passage. List them here:

✦ Label this diagram.

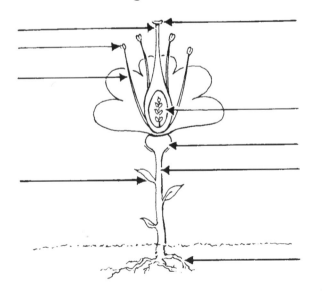

✦ Complete this table.

female parts	male parts	other parts

Developing
literacy
Skills

Photocopiable

◆ Flowering plants ◆

◆ You are going to make some notes about flowering plants. Read the information then complete the tasks.

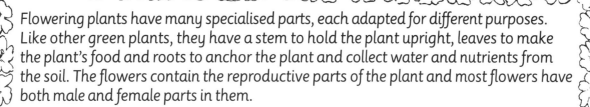

Flowering plants have many specialised parts, each adapted for different purposes. Like other green plants, they have a stem to hold the plant upright, leaves to make the plant's food and roots to anchor the plant and collect water and nutrients from the soil. The flowers contain the reproductive parts of the plant and most flowers have both male and female parts in them.

Pollination must take place before the flower can reproduce itself. Pollen needs to be transferred from the male part of one flower to the female part of another flower of the same species. This transfer can be carried out by insects, birds or wind. Insects are attracted to flowers by the brightly coloured petals and scent. Pollen collects on their bodies as they drink nectar from the flower and then some falls off again when they visit another flower.

The female part is called the pistil. It is usually found in the centre of the flower and has a top called a stigma, a long tube called a style and a bulbous base called the ovary. Inside the ovary are many eggs. The male parts surround the pistil. They are called stamens and have a anther at the top and a long stem called a filament. The pollen is found on the anther.

When pollen from a neighbouring plant lands on the stigma, it grows a tube into the ovary where it combines with the egg and fertilises it. The egg then grows into a seed.

◆ Circle the names of all the different plant parts mentioned in the passage. Use these words to draw and label a diagram of a flowering plant here.

◆ On the back of this page, draw up a table and list words under the following headings: male parts, female parts, other parts.

Overall aims

- To read and evaluate letters which use persuasive writing to express a point of view.
- To explore how language is used to express opinion and bias, gain attention and persuade.
- To write letters which express a point of view.

 ### Suggested texts

A collection of letters to the Editor from newspapers.

 ### LESSON ONE

 ### Intended learning

- To read and evaluate letters which contain persuasive writing.
- To discuss terms such as fact, opinion, bias, persuasion and ambiguity.

Today's Farms are Best!

How wonderful it was to read Mr Pearce's letter about modern farming methods! (*Daily Post*, July 17) He no doubt has all the answers I need to make my farm a better place! And where does Mr Pearce live I wonder? Oh yes, right in the centre of Birmingham, just the right place to learn all about life on a farm!

I have been farming for 40 years. My father was here until he died at 85 and his father farmed our property before that, so I think I'm in a much better position than Mr Pearce to comment about modern farming methods. Farming today is much kinder to animals and that's a fact! My cattle get the very best of feed, exercise, human attention and veterinary care so I want to say to all of you out there – talk to us farmers before you make sweeping statements about farms today!

John Dunn
Downend Farm

 ### Starting point: Whole class

- **Photocopy and enlarge the letter below left so that each child has a copy.**
- Discuss the meaning of the terms 'fact', 'opinion', 'ambiguity', 'bias' and 'persuasion', providing the children with examples.

 ### Group activities

- Answer the following questions about the letter:
  - Did Mr Dunn really think Mr Pearce's letter was wonderful or is this an example of ambiguity?
  - Can you find other examples of ambiguity?
  - What information in the letter do you consider to be fact?
  - What information in the letter do you consider to be opinion?
  - Has Mr Dunn assumed anything about Mr Pearce? What?
  - Do you consider Mr Dunn's letter to show bias? If so, how?
  - What do you think of the letter's title? Is it an appropriate one or not? Explain why.
- Provide examples of letters written to newspapers. Ask them to sort them into two piles – ones they agree with and ones they do not. Tell them to select one letter from each pile and write down their reasons for agreeing or disagreeing with it.

 ### Plenary session

Share the responses to the questions about the farming letter. Is there agreement? What effect does ambiguity create in the letter? Why is this technique used? Is it deliberate? Evaluate the letter – do they think it has been well written or not? Why? Select some of the other letters from newspapers to share. Listen to some of the children's reasons for agreeing or disagreeing with them. Discuss how language can be used to persuade, grab attention, complain and give an opinion. Has opinion been disguised to seem like fact? How credible do they think the letters are?

 **LESSON TWO**

Intended learning

✦ To write a letter which expresses a point of view.

Starting point: Whole class

✦ Remind the children about the farming letter discussed in Lesson 1. Tell them that they are now going to help write a letter to the editor of the newspaper in response to that letter.

✦ Discuss and model the correct layout of a formal letter. Use the school address on the right-hand side and make up an address for the newspaper to be presented on the left-hand side. Discuss how the date can be set out and how to address and end a formal letter.

✦ Ask the children to pretend that they are going to reply to the letter disagreeing with Mr Dunn, the farmer. Issues which could be mentioned in the letter include battery-hen farming, BSE crisis, use of chemicals and so on. Decide which issue(s) will be used and then talk about the type of language that might be used in the letter.

✦ Agree on a good beginning – how can we grab the reader's attention? What facts could we include? What opinions will we give? Can bias be avoided? Model writing, editing and re-drafting the letter until everyone is happy with the result.

✦ Explain that they will now have an opportunity to practise writing their own letter using the class example as a model. Talk through the activity with them beforehand. Explain that letters to the editor are written like normal letters but the newspaper sets them out in a different format – they give the letter a heading and do not give the sender's full address without permission. Remind the children to check through their letters carefully when finished, perhaps working with a partner to edit and review them.

Using the differentiated activity sheets

Activity sheet 1

This activity is for children who need more support with setting out a letter. The children are required to give their opinion on a simple, familiar issue.

Activity sheet 2

This activity is for children who are more confident letter writers. They are required to give an opinion on a more complicated issue.

Activity sheet 3

This activity is for more able children. It requires them to give an opinion on a very topical and emotive issue.

 Plenary session

After the children have completed their letters, bring the whole class together again. Remind the children about the correct setting out of a formal letter and ask them to refer to their letters to check layout. Ask some children from each group to read out their letters. Is it clear what their point of view is? Have they referred to the newspaper article? Does the letter contain facts or just opinion? Does it grab people's attention? How? Is bias evident? Has persuasive language been used? Is the letter interesting and relevant?

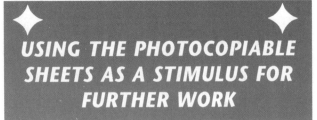

Letters

USING THE PHOTOCOPIABLE SHEETS AS A STIMULUS FOR FURTHER WORK

✦ Ask the children from each group to prepare a debate about the issue presented on their activity sheet – some children for and some against.

✦ Use reference books, newspapers and fliers to find out more information about the issues. Encourage the children to find out about both sides of the argument. Use a desktop publishing program to design a leaflet that presents both sides of the issue.

✦ Ask the children using Activity sheet 1 to make 3-D models of lunches – good and poor school dinners as well as good and poor packed lunches. Write information about each lunch, explaining why they are good or poor.

✦ Ask the children using Activity sheet 2 to make up two advertisements – one for radio (advertising the benefits of radio over television) and one for television (advertising the benefits of television). Act them out.

✦ Ask the children using Activity sheet 3 to design two posters – one for and one against hunting and fishing.

✦ Build up a word bank of emotive and persuasive words that could be used to sway people's opinion. Start with the words used in the letters and use dictionaries and thesauruses to find more.

✦ Carry out surveys to find out people's opinions about the issues in the activity sheets.

OTHER IDEAS FOR USING LETTERS

✦ Read local newspapers and write letters for a real purpose about a local issue and post them to the newspaper.

✦ Make a collection of business letters. Compare how they are set out – make aesthetic judgements and give reasons for choices. Compare letterhead designs. Make up letterheads for the school or a fictitious company.

✦ Set up a class business. Write letters to the children, such as job application acceptances and work to be commissioned. Ask the children to reply to the letters then carry out the tasks you ask them to do in your answering letter.

✦ Send off real letters in response to advertising features, such as products relating to the class topic. Write back thank you letters after receiving the goods.

✦ Visit the local postal sorting office to find out how letters are processed. Make flow diagrams of the steps involved.

✦ Explore connecting words and phrases used in persuasive letters, such as 'therefore', 'however', 'nevertheless' and 'whereas'. Make a list to display as a reference guide for letter writing.

✦ Write fictitious letters of complaint. Ask others to reply to the letters.

✦ School dinners ✦

✦ You are going to write a letter to the editor of a newspaper in reply to this reader's comment about school dinners. Remember to write about your own views as well as commenting on things Simon Brown has said.

School Dinners are Best!
Nothing can beat a school dinner! I love my school dinners and I have them every day. The food is lovely. We often have chips and I love chips so I always have them. I can leave anything I don't want on the plate and mum never knows that I didn't eat my peas! I can have seconds of puddings if I want to and I usually do. I feel sorry for the kids who have lunches from home because they don't get hot tasty food like I do.

Simon Brown, Park St Juniors

The Editor,
Hillstreet News,
News Street,
Wonderton
WT 5 2 HN

Dear Sir/Madam,

← write your school address and today's date here

Yours faithfully,

sign your name at the bottom.

✦ Check through your letter carefully. Does it make sense? Have you put in capital letters and full stops? Use a dictionary to check your spellings.

◆ Television ◆

◆ Write a letter to the editor of a newspaper in reply to this reader's comments about television. Do you agree or disagree with the comments? Write down your views in your letter as well as commenting on the things Mrs Sythe has said.

Children Watch Too Much Television

Children today watch far too much television. They don't get enough exercise and they always seem bored. In my day we were never bored, we always found something to do. We used to invent games that kept us outside for hours. Yet today all the kids seem to want to do is sit in front of the telly.

They watch all the wrong programmes too and I'm sure this has a bad effect on them. Parents should control what their children watch instead of letting them go up to their bedrooms where they can turn on their own set and watch programmes which are just not suitable. All the violence, burglary and vandalism in our area is caused by kids copying what they see on TV. Parents – please take note and do something before it's too late!

Mrs J Sythe, Ashburton Estate

◆ Write your letter here:

The Editor
Hillstreet News
News Street
Wonderton
WT5 2HN

◆ Does your letter make sense? Check your spelling and punctuation.

Developing
literacy
Skills

◆ Hunting and fishing ◆

◆ You are going to write a letter to the editor of a newspaper in reply to this reader's comments about hunting and fishing. Do you agree or disagree with the comments? Write down your views in your letter as well as commenting on the things John Wood has said.

◆ Write your letter here. Use the back of this page if you need more space.

Angler Fights Back!

Has the whole world gone mad? Have the anti's got nothing better to do on a peaceful Sunday than to invade our beautiful river bank and try and prevent us fishermen from enjoying an ancient pastime? I was appalled by what happened to me and my friends last week. We were quietly fishing when all of a sudden we were set upon by a bunch of maniacs who want fishing and hunting of any kind banned. They broke our fishing rods and threw away our bait. What right have these people to do that? There are lots of things in this world I don't agree with but I don't go around hurting people and damaging property! Why can't these people just let others enjoy their hobbies while they enjoy theirs? I always put back the fish I catch and they're never harmed. The ones I do keep, I eat – after all, we've got to eat something! Leave us alone to fish in peace!

John Wood, Melville Place

The Editor
Hillstreet News
News Street
Wonderton
WT5 2HN

Dictionaries

Overall aims

- To explore different types of dictionaries to discuss purpose and organisation.
- To use dictionaries to explore spellings and meanings.

Suggested texts

A variety of different dictionaries, such as dictionaries of phrases, quotations, synonyms, antonyms, thesauruses and subject-based dictionaries.

LESSON ONE

Intended learning

- To become familiar with a range of dictionaries and their uses.
- To examine how information is organised and presented.
- To practise using dictionaries efficiently.

Starting point: Whole class

- Show the children different types of dictionaries. Read out the titles and ask them to tell you what kinds of things they think will be inside the dictionaries. Why do they think there is such a huge variety? Why are specialist dictionaries such as science dictionaries needed, for example?
- Ask them to tell you how dictionaries are used. Revise the use of guide words at the top of pages and how to scan pages using the first three or more letters to find the word.
- Practise these skills by providing a copy of the same page from a dictionary. Race to find particular words on the page.
- Next, look at the way the information is presented. Discuss the use of parentheses, italics, pronunciation, abbreviations for parts of speech and word origins and so on, using the words on the page as examples.

- Go through the layout of a dictionary, showing them the pages where the abbreviations and symbols used in the book are explained, the key to pronunications and any other information provided. Demonstrate how to read the entries. Practise finding words in the dictionary, looking at not only the definition given but the symbols and abbreviations used. Discuss how to cross-reference words from one part of the same dictionary to another or to another dictionary.

Group activities

- Divide the children into small groups. Provide them with a different kind of dictionary each. Ask them to investigate how information is presented by answering the following questions:
  - What information is provided in the introductory pages?
  - How are the guide words organised – two words at the top of each page or two words at the top of a double page?
  - Does the dictionary have illustrations or diagrams?
  - Does the dictionary have extra information at the back of the book? If so, what?
  - Does the book use parentheses, abbreviations and give parts of speech and word origins?
  - Is cross-referencing used? (Does the dictionary say see... for some entries?)
  - How is word pronunciation demonstrated?

Plenary session

Bring the whole class together again and ask several children from each group to report back on the answers to the questions in relation to the dictionary they used. What are the similarities and differences between the dictionaries? Which dictionary would the children prefer to use? Why? What difficulties did the children have in using the dictionary? Discuss ways of overcoming these problems.

Dictionaries

LESSON TWO

◆ Intended learning

◆ To use dictionaries to explore spellings and meanings.
◆ To investigate antonyms and synonyms.

◆ Starting point: Whole class

◆ Provide the children with a thesaurus each or one between two. Ask them to tell you what kind of dictionary a thesaurus is.
◆ Look at the content together, noting what information is given in the introduction and how the book is organised. Demonstrate how to use the thesaurus to find specific words.
◆ Explain the terms 'synonym' and 'antonym'. Ask the children to tell you some synonyms and antonyms for common words, without using the thesaurus.
◆ Then use the thesaurus to find particular words. Discuss how it provides many meanings for the one word and how it is necessary to find the most appropriate word for the purpose.
◆ Demonstrate how to cross-check words when the listed words are not known to the children. For example, when looking up 'noisy', the word 'cacophanous' might be listed. The children then might need to look up 'cacophanous' in a dictionary to cross-check its meaning.
◆ Discuss how the organisation and content of a thesaurus differs from an ordinary dictionary.

◆ Using the differentiated activity sheets

Activity sheet 1

This activity sheet is aimed at those children who need more support with dictionary work. The words and tasks are simpler.

Activity sheet 2

This activity sheet is for children who are confident users of dictionaries.

Activity sheet 3

This activity sheet is aimed at more able children. The words and tasks are more difficult and should challenge even the best of spellers!

Plenary session

Bring the whole class together again when the children have completed the sheets. Discuss the meanings of the 're' words on all sheets and explain that the prefix 're' comes from Latin and means again or back. Ask one or two children from each group to share one word which has been incorrectly spelled. Do others know the correct spelling? Share some of the synonyms and antonyms. Ask the children to tell you the meaning of a word which was new to them today. Remind the children how useful thesauruses can be when drafting and editing writing tasks.

Dictionaries

USING THE PHOTOCOPIABLE SHEETS AS A STIMULUS FOR FURTHER WORK

- Explore the prefix 're' further. Find other 're' words. Use the words in sentences to show their meaning. Make a dictionary of 're' words.

- Write alliterations using the 're' words.

- Make a book of antonyms and/or synonyms, beginning with the words on the activity sheets.

- Make a class list of 'tricky' spellings, beginning with those on the sheets. Display them as a spelling resource.

- Make up crossword puzzles or word searches using words on the sheets to reinforce spelling knowledge.

- Make a class thesaurus of words relating to the class topic to aid writing tasks.

- Ask the children to write definitions of some of the words on their sheets. Check with dictionaries to compare definitions.

- Challenge the children to write the longest sentence they can using words from the sheets.

- Explore other prefixes. Change the meaning of words by adding prefixes, such as slave, enslave and grain, ingrain. Find out the meaning of Latin, Greek and Anglo-Saxon prefixes.

OTHER IDEAS FOR USING DICTIONARIES

- Use dictionaries to explore word derivations.

- Make class dictionaries that are subject-based, such as a science dictionary. Illustrate them with diagrams.

- Investigate 'new' words that have entered our language. Make up a dictionary of modern and/or colloquial words to enlighten parents!

- Use old dictionaries to find out how the meaning of words have changed, such as 'gay' and 'wicked'.

- Make up crossword puzzles or quizzes where the children have to use a specific dictionary to find the answers.

- Have a 'Word of the day'. Encourage the children to find out its meaning and use the word throughout the day in conversations.

- Have fun finding the longest words. Challenge the children to use dictionaries to find the longest word for each letter of the alphabet.

- Make up simple dictionaries in other languages – use those languages spoken by children at school or French and German.

◆ Using dictionaries ◆

◆ Write these words in dictionary order. Use a dictionary to see if you are correct.

remake refund renew recall review recover return recycle remind repeat

_____

_____

◆ None of these words are spelled correctly.
   Use a dictionary to find the correct spellings.

word	definition	correct spelling
Febuary	second month of the year	
neccesary	needed to do something	
caterpiller	larva of a butterfly	
wierd	very strange	
pjamas	clothes worn in bed	

◆ Use a thesaurus to write a synonym and antonym for these words.

word	synonym	antonym
merry		
enter		
ready		
alone		
pale		

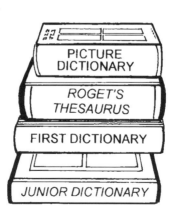

PICTURE
DICTIONARY

ROGET'S
THESAURUS

FIRST DICTIONARY

JUNIOR DICTIONARY

Photocopiable

©Hopscotch Educational Publishing

◆ Using dictionaries ◆

◆Write these words in dictionary order. Use a dictionary to see if you are correct.

regain retain rebound rejoin reclaim repeat regress recoil rehash recur

_____

_____

◆Ten of these words are not spelled correctly. Circle the ones you think are incorrect.
Use a dictionary to write the correct spellings underneath the words.

dissapear	eighth	embarrassed	humourous
	parallell	picnicking	mischievious
chimney	professor	begining	ocassionally
	seperate	rythm	omitted
comittee	foreign	parliament	stoping

◆Use a thesaurus to write 3 synonyms and 3 antonyms for these words.

word	synonyms	antonyms
savage		
dreary		
extraordinary		
perfect		
abundant		
immense		
ridiculous		

38

Using non-fiction
KS2: Y5–6/P6–7

Developing
literacy
Skills

Photocopiable

©Hopscotch Educational Publishing

✦ Using dictionaries ✦

✦ Write these words in dictionary order. Use a dictionary to see if you are correct.

repossess regenerate reimburse revive reiterate retrieve regurgitate reincarnate relapse reproduce

_____

_____

✦ Put a tick next to the words below that you think are spelled correctly. Use a dictionary to write the correct spellings of the incorrect words.

accidently	accommodation	alright
auxiliary	bouyant	cemetary
competition	conscientious	deceive
definate	develope	disapointed
enviroment	exaggerate	familiar
freind	goverment	height
humorous	immediately	laboratory
litrature	lonley	marriage
occurred	pronounciation	referred
restaurant	suprise	villan

✦ Use a thesaurus to find the most appropriate synonym for these words.

inarticulate _____

prejudice _____

conspicuous _____

gnarled _____

miniature _____

blatant _____

theoretical _____

haphazard _____

shrewd _____

✦ Use a thesaurus to find the most appropriate antonym for these words.

dominant _____

negative _____

connect _____

knowledge _____

secretive _____

vicious _____

effervescent _____

natural _____

turbulent _____

Biographies and autobiographies

Overall aims

- To explore the characteristics of autobiographical and biographical writing.
- To discuss the differences between fact, fiction and opinion.
- To write in autobiographical and biographical styles.

Suggested texts

A Picture Book of Anne Frank by David A Adler (Puffin) and *The Diary of a Young Girl* by Anne Frank (edited by Otto H Frank and Mirjam Pressler, translated by Susan Massotty, Macmillan).

LESSON ONE

Intended learning

- To explore the characteristics of autobiographical and biographical writing.
- To discuss the differences between fact, fiction and opinion.

Starting point: Whole class

- Ask the children to tell you if they have heard of Anne Frank. Briefly outline how she became so well-known and then share the picture book with the class.
- Explain that this book is a biography. Discuss the meaning of the term. Have the children read any other biographies?
- Show them the book written by Anne Frank. Explain that this book is an autobiography and discuss the meaning of this term.
- Read some paragraphs from the Saturday, 20th June, 1942 pages in the book and ask the children to tell you some of the ways in which the writing styles in the two books differ. Talk about the use of first person and third person and how the writing of a diary differs from a biography. How might a newspaper article about Anne Frank differ from these two accounts? What might be different about the language used?

- Discuss the meanings of the terms 'fact', 'fiction' and 'opinion' in relation to the biography, diary and a newspaper report about Anne Frank. Which account would contain the most reliable facts about Anne Frank? Why?
- Discuss whether autobiographies and biographies can be fictional (*The Secret Diary of Adrian Mole aged 13 3/4* by Sue Townsend).
- Finally, draw up a class list of the differences between an autobiography and a biography.

Activities

- Using extracts from the biography of Anne Frank, ask the children to write down five facts about Anne and then five sentences giving their own opinions about her.
- Ask them to underline the facts and opinions in an extract from the diary (for example, Friday 5th February 1943).
- Ask them to compare the descriptions of going into hiding in the two books (Wednesday 8th July 1942). Ask them to write down how they think they would feel if it was happening to them. What things would they take with them?

Plenary session

Bring the whole class together again when the children have completed the activities. Compare the lists of facts and opinions. Do others agree? Compare answers to the last activity. Discuss how the children might feel if it was happening to them and what they might take with them. Do the children think it was a good idea to have the diary published? Why? What purposes can there be for publishing biographies and autobiographies? How can these types of books help us?

©Hopscotch Educational Publishing

Developing literacy Skills

Using non-fiction

◆ LESSON TWO ◆

◆ Intended learning

◆ To write in autobiographical and biographical styles.

◆ Starting point: Whole class

◆ Ask the children to remind you of the meaning of the terms biography and autobiography. Can they remember some of the differences in writing styles used?

◆ Explain that they will have an opportunity to write in the style of an autobiography and a biography in this lesson.

◆ Write a list of facts about a real or fictional person on the board. Include name, date and place of birth, family details, events that happened to the person and so on.

◆ Ask the children to look at the list and imagine that they are this person. How might they begin writing a paragraph about themselves? Model writing an autobiography, using the list to write sentences. Discuss the use of first person, correct tense and phrases that might be used to describe personal feelings.

◆ Next, model a paragraph written as a biography, using the same information. Can the children suggest how it might begin? Discuss the use of third person and correct tense.

◆ Compare the two pieces of writing. Are the children satisfied that they successfully represent a biography and an autobiography? Why?

◆ Explain that they are now going to carry out the same writing tasks using information about the Murray family who lived during World War II. If necessary, provide reference books about life in Britain during World War II to help them appreciate what life may have been like for the Murray's at that time in history.

◆ Using the differentiated activity sheets

Each activity sheet concerns itself with a different member of the Murray family. The children are required to write in autobiographical and biographical styles.

Activity sheet 1

This is aimed at those children who need support with their writing. It is presented as a cloze activity.

Activity sheet 2

This is for more confident writers. The children may need reminding to write in sentences, not note form.

Activity sheet 3

This is for more able children. They will need to share copies of Activity sheets 1 and 2 in order to find out facts such as when Peter Murray married and when he could have been born. They need to consider the type of work he did before and during the war and whether or not he lived in London or was sent away. Reference books will be vital to this group and they may benefit from working in pairs or as a small group.

◆ Plenary session

Bring the whole class together again when the children have completed the tasks. Ask some children from each group to read out the autobiography and biography for each member of the Murray family. How many different possibilities are there for the cloze activities in order for the sentences to still make sense? Could the facts for Mr Murray be true? How well did the children in this group do their research? Compare the writing styles used – are they appropriate for the task? Did the children find it difficult to imagine they were someone else? Which type of writing was easiest to do? Why?

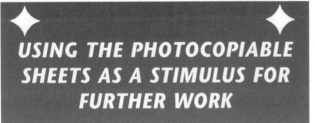

Biographies and autobiographies

◆ USING THE PHOTOCOPIABLE SHEETS AS A STIMULUS FOR FURTHER WORK

✦ Ask the children to write a diary for each member of the Murray family, using reference books for guidance. How might their character feel and behave? What things might happen to them in their daily lives – how might they feel about these?

✦ Discuss the lives of Richard Murray and Anne Frank. How different were their experiences of war?

✦ Make up a class 'photo album' about the Murray family. Ask the children to draw 'photographs' about the Murrays and write captions to go with them.

✦ Find out more information about the lives of men, women and children during the war. Use the information to write a class book about home and school life, rationing, air-raid shelters and so on.

✦ Ask the children to prepare a talk, pretending they are one of the Murray's. Ask them to talk about one aspect of their lives, such as 'keeping a home together', 'what it is like to be evacuated' or 'my life as a soldier'.

✦ Make a class mural of the Murray family with paintings and writing about them. Ask the children to do a poster about their own family to go with the display in order to compare life then and now.

✦ Look at ID cards used during the war. Use these to model writing some ID cards for each member of the Murray family.

✦ Write poems about each member of the Murray family. Build up a collection of war-time poems to make a class display.

◆ OTHER IDEAS FOR USING BIOGRAPHIES AND AUTOBIOGRAPHIES

✦ Ask the children to work in pairs. They each write a list of facts about themselves. Take it in turns to read out the facts to the partner who then has to use this information to write his/her partner's biography.

✦ Write biographies of historical people encountered in class topic work.

✦ Ask the children to write their own 'CV' (invented or real). Use the CVs to hold mock interviews – for a television talk-show, a radio programme or a newspaper report.

✦ Make up police descriptions of 'wanted' people. Ask the children to use the information to write a biography of the wanted person to be placed in a police file.

✦ Read the children biographies and autobiographies, both real and imagined, in order to widen their experiences of the two writing styles.

✦ Investigate how the lives of famous people are presented in newspapers and magazines. Can we believe what we read? Discuss bias and opinion. Compare 'facts' in journalistic writing with 'facts' from a biography about the same person.

✦ Write journals at school to encourage the children to write about their feelings and experiences.

◆ Richard Murray ◆

◆Write an autobiography and biography about Richard Murray.

Richard Murray

born July 12th, 1930	lived at Seaton with with Mr and Mrs Pitt
born in London	helped Mr Pitt in grocery shop
evacuated to Seaton, Cumbria in 1940	
first visited sea-side June 9th 1940	returned to London in 1942

◆ Pretend that you are Richard Murray. Use the information above to complete this autobiography.

◆ Now use the same information to complete this biography of Richard Murray.

I was born in _____ on _____ 1930. I lived in _____ with my _____ until 1940 when I was evacuated to _____ in _____. I was very _____ when I left _____ to travel to Seaton. We went there by _____. It was the first time I had been on a train and I felt very _____. When I _____ in Seaton, I was met by Mr and _____ who were going to look after me. Mr Seaton owned a _____ shop and I helped him there every day after _____. On June 9th _____ I had the best experience of my _____ because I went to the _____ for the very first time ever! It was _____. I returned home to _____ in _____.

Richard _____ was born in _____ on _____ 1930. He lived there with his _____ until _____ when he was evacuated to _____ in Cumbria. The war forced many children like _____ to leave their _____ to find safety in the countryside. Richard had never been on a _____ before so he found the trip very _____. Mr and Mrs ____ met Richard when he arrived in _____. He was to stay with the Pitts for a couple of _____. Richard had never seen the _____ before so he was very _____ when he finally spent a whole day there on _____. Richard used to help Mr Pitt in his _____ shop after school. He finally returned to London in _____.

Developing Literacy Skills

◆ Mrs Murray ◆

◆ Write a biography and autobiography about Mrs Murray.

Mrs Jean Murray

born in Chelmsford, Essex

worked as a secretary

moved to London in 1928

joined the WVS (Women's Voluntary Service) in 1939

knitted socks for soldiers

sent Richard to safety in Seaton in 1940

born 2nd December, 1910

married Peter Murray on July 12th 1928

son, Richard born July 12th, 1930

helped other women in WVS to look after people whose homes had been bombed

used the underground as an air-raid shelter at night

◆ Pretend that you are Mrs Murray. Use the information above to write an autobiography. Write about her feelings and concerns as well as the facts.

◆ Now use the same information to write a biography about Mrs Murray.

◆ Continue on the back of this sheet.

Developing
literacy
Skills

Activity 3

◆ Mr Murray ◆

◆ This is Peter Murray. Use the facts from Activity sheets 1 and 2 as well as information books to make up a list of possible facts about him.

Facts about Mr Murray

◆ Pretend you are Mr Murray. Use the facts above to write your autobiography.

◆ Now use the same information to write a biography about Mr Murray.

◆ Continue on the back of this sheet.

Using non-fiction
KS2: Y5–6/P6–7

Developing
literacy
Skills

Photocopiable
©Hopscotch Educational Publishing
45

Overall aims

✦ To explore the structure of writing which expresses the pros and cons of an issue.
✦ To explore the meaning of bias and opinion.
✦ To use notes to write an argument for and against an issue.

 Suggested texts

A collection of leaflets, information sheets, fliers and notices which express a point of view.

 **LESSON ONE**

 Intended learning

✦ To explore the structure of writing which expresses the pros and cons of an issue.
✦ To explore the meaning of bias and opinion.

 Starting point: Whole class

✦ Show the children the collection of leaflets and information sheets. Explain that information about issues and events are often presented in this format so they can be pasted on walls, put up in shop windows, posted to households or handed out at meetings. Explain that the purpose of the information is often to persuade the reader towards a particular point of view – it presents an opinion. The information might then be biased. Discuss the terms bias and opinion.

✦ Provide the children with a photocopy of the texts at the bottom of this page.
✦ Discuss the bias and opinions presented in each text. Talk about the persuasive and emotive language used such as: 'Any intelligent person…', 'the real truth is…', 'that's a fact', 'you can't afford to miss out…' and 'the nation's favourite…'.
✦ Explore the type of connectives used in the arguments, such as: 'firstly', 'so', 'therefore', 'whereas' and 'surely'.
✦ Explain that they will now have an opportunity to examine the arguments presented further.

 Group activities

✦ Working in pairs, ask the children to write up a list of the pros and cons for having a new supermarket built, based on the evidence in the texts.
✦ Evaluate the arguments. Which argument are you most persuaded by? Write down your reasons why. How could the arguments be improved?

 Plenary session

Bring the whole class together again to share their ideas. Compare lists of pros and cons – is there agreement? Which argument do most of the class agree with? Ask for reasons why. Discuss improving the texts – could more information be given? What better/ more persuasive words and phrases could be used? Have enough facts been included?

Say NO to the Supermarket!
Do we need yet another supermarket? Any intelligent person would say no! Why? Well firstly, we already have a supermarket in the area so people can use that one. Secondly, we need all the green spaces we can get! Some of our lovely playing fields have already gone for housing so we don't want to lose any more for the sake of a supermarket. The real truth is we don't need another supermarket and that's a fact! Therefore fight with us against the planned supermarket – for all our sakes!

Exciting NEW Supermarket!
The nation's favourite supermarket is planned to open near you soon. Yes, that's right, you will no longer have to travel miles because the very best will soon be available right on your doorstep. We aim to build a brand new shopping complex with free parking, an adventure playground and free creche facilities. We are going to provide an hourly free bus service to our store. Surely you can't afford to miss out on all these advantages, so make sure you support us!

46
©Hopscotch Educational Publishing

 Developing
literacy
Skills

Using non-fiction
KS2: Y5–6/P6–7

Arguments

◆ LESSON TWO ◆

◆ Intended learning

◆ To use notes to write an argument for and against an issue.

◆ Starting point: Whole class

◆ Ask the children to remind you about the two texts explored in Lesson 1. Explain that they are going to prepare an argument for and against building new supermarkets. Discuss what the term argument means.

◆ Make up a class list of reasons for and reasons against building a supermarket – include those from Lesson 1's texts and others the children think of themselves.

◆ Model how to use the list to write an argument in sentence form. Discuss the use of third person rather than first. Talk about having a balance of fact and opinion in the argument.

◆ Discuss and evaluate the draft and revise it together to improve clarity, balance and objectivity.

◆ Explain that they will now have an opportunity to carry out the same task in relation to some different issues.

◆ Using the differentiated activity sheets

Activity sheet 1

This activity sheet is aimed at those children who need more support to write an argument. The notes on the page are written in sentences to help them when they write their own. It may be best for children in this group to work in pairs.

Activity sheet 2

This activity is aimed at those children who are more confident writers. Some reasons for and against the issue are given but there is also an opportunity for the children to add their own. The list is written in note form and the children are required to use the notes to write full sentences.

Activity sheet 3

This activity is aimed at more able children as it requires them to think of their own list of reasons for and against. These children may need to use reference books to find out information about the health risks of smoking.

◆ Plenary session

Bring the whole class together again when the children have completed their arguments. Explain each task and ask several people from each group to share their arguments for or against the issue. How coherent are the arguments? Are there any contradictions or ambiguities? Are the arguments balanced? Which argument are they most convinced by? Why?

Arguments

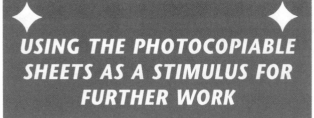

USING THE PHOTOCOPIABLE SHEETS AS A STIMULUS FOR FURTHER WORK

✦ Ask the children to plan a campaign in relation to the issue on their activity sheet. They could design fliers or information leaflets for and against the issue. Discuss layout, use of illustrations/diagrams and the amount of information to use. Use desktop publishing programs to create a professional finish. Bumper stickers, advertising posters, T-shirts and other merchandise could also be designed.

✦ They could use their writing to prepare for a group debate to be performed in front of the whole class.

✦ Use information books, newspapers and other sources of reference to find out more information about the issues.

✦ Ask the children to devise a television or radio advertisement to make people aware of the issue. Act them out.

✦ Contact organisations concerned with each issue. Write letters to find out the answers to questions the children raise.

✦ Make up secret codes so campaigners can talk to each other secretly!

✦ How convincing can you be? Ask the children to give a talk for or against an issue. Can the others guess if these are the person's real beliefs or not?

✦ Conduct a survey across the whole school to find out what others think about the three issues.

✦ Challenge the children to turn reasons for an issue into reasons against. For example, you can wear different clothes every day (reason for not having a school uniform), but your clothes soon wear out (reason against).

OTHER IDEAS FOR USING ARGUMENTS

✦ Practise debating regularly to give the children a chance to express their opinions in a structured way and to develop public speaking skills.

✦ Make a scrapbook of newspaper and magazine articles relating to specific issues. Use the book to promote class discussions about current issues and to study how journalistic writing is used to present an argument.

✦ Use magazine advertisements to discuss fact and opinion and use of persuasion. Discuss the influence advertisements have on our lives.

✦ Make a class collection of poems which express an opinion. Ask the children to write their own poem in response to a particular one.

✦ Study political cartoons from newspapers. Write a cartoon which expresses an opinion.

✦ Share stories such as *When the Wind Blows* by Raymond Briggs to provide a basis for debate and developing arguments.

✦ Ask the children to write personal viewpoints, such as: 'Why I believe in Ghosts'. Share the writing. Are others convinced by the reasons given?

Activity 1

◆ School uniform ◆

✦ Read the notes on having a school uniform below.
Underline in red the sentences that give reasons for having a uniform.
Underline in blue the sentences against having a uniform.

> *You can wear different clothes every day.*
> > *You can be more individual.*
> *It makes you feel proud of your school.*
> > *It saves money.*
> *It's not comfortable to wear.*
> > *It's comfortable.*
> *You don't have to decide what to wear.*
> > *You feel like you belong to a group.*
> *It looks good on school outings.*
> > *You can keep your clothes for weekends.*
> *It looks good.*
> > *You know which clothes are yours.*
> *It's expensive.*
> > *The colour might not suit everyone.*

✦ Use the sentences underlined in red to write an argument for having a school uniform here.

✦ Use the sentences underlined in blue to write an argument against having a school uniform here.

✦ Check through your writing carefully. Does it make sense? Have you used capital letters and full stops? Use a dictionary to check spellings.

Developing
literacy
Skills

◆ Cars ◆

◆ Read these notes on reasons for and against owning a car. Add four or
more other reasons of your own to each column.

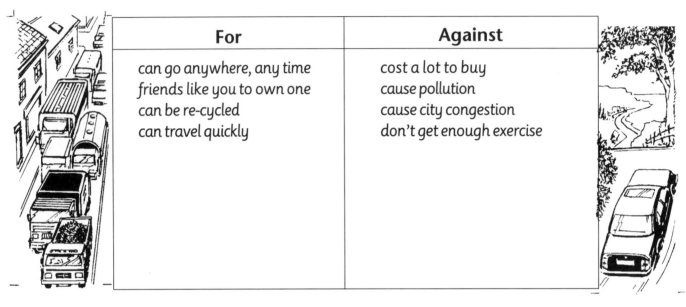

For	Against
can go anywhere, any time friends like you to own one can be re-cycled can travel quickly	cost a lot to buy cause pollution cause city congestion don't get enough exercise

◆ Use these notes to write an argument for and against owning cars.
Write your arguments in sentences.

For:

Against:

◆ Check through your writing carefully. Does it make sense? Is the punctuation correct?
Use a dictionary to check spellings.

◆ Smoking ◆

◆ Think about the reasons for and against smoking. List your reasons below.

For	Against

◆ Use your lists to write an argument for and against smoking. Write your arguments in sentences.

For:

Against:

◆ Check through your writing carefully. Does it make sense? Is the punctuation correct?
  Use a dictionary to check spellings.

Official forms

◆ Overall aims

- ✦ To discuss examples of official language used in forms.
- ✦ To investigate the layout and special features of forms.
- ✦ To write a report in response to a form.

◆ Suggested texts

A collection of different examples of official forms such as applications for a junior bank account or passport, consumer surveys, job applications, loan agreements and so on.

◆ LESSON ONE ◆

◆ Intended learning

- ✦ To discuss examples of official language used in forms.
- ✦ To investigate the layout and special features of forms.

◆ Starting point: Whole class

- ✦ Ask the children to tell you whether or not they have ever filled in a form. For what purpose? Have their parents had to complete some forms recently? Make a list of things you might need to complete a form for.
- ✦ Ask the children if they or their parents had any problems when completing the forms. What kind of problems were they? Are forms always easy to complete?
- ✦ Provide the children with a copy of the same form(s) each (perhaps an application for a bank account or passport). Ask them to quickly scan the form to see if they come across anything they do not understand or would find difficult to do. Discuss the meanings of any unknown terms, such as 'maiden name', 'dependants', 'marital status', 'country of origin' and so on. Talk about ways of finding out necessary answers.

- ✦ Ask the children to tell you what is different about the language used in forms, compared with a story book, for example. Note the features of official form language such as specialist language, impersonal voice, use of imperative and so on.
- ✦ Discuss the layout of the form – use of instructions, parentheses, headings, numbering, footnotes, boxes and expressions, such as: 'if yes, go to...' and 'please tick those that apply'.
- ✦ Explain that many people often find forms difficult to fill in and therefore it is important to read the instructions carefully before beginning the task.

◆ Activities

- ✦ Ask the children to complete the form(s)!
- ✦ Ask them to look at a collection of different forms and select one they consider has the best layout. Ask them to write down four reasons for selecting this form.
- ✦ Provide a particularly detailed form and ask them to work in pairs to suggest ways of making the form easier to use or read.
- ✦ Ask the children to make a tally of the types of information asked for – which information do ALL the forms require?

◆ Plenary session

Bring the whole class together when the children have completed the tasks. How difficult was it to complete the form(s)? What information would they need to find out from parents? Which layout is best? Is there class agreement? What makes the chosen form better than the others? What makes a 'bad' form? Too much text, too small print? Do tick boxes help? What information is required on all the forms – name, address, telephone number, date of birth? Discuss why forms are necessary – could the information be gained or presented in any other way? Is confidentiality important? What might happen to the information?

Official forms

◆ LESSON TWO ◆

◆ Intended learning

◆ To write a report in response to a form.

◆ Starting point: Whole class

◆ Remind the children about the discussions about forms in Lesson 1. Explain that once forms have been completed it is someone's task to use the information for a particular purpose. A bank, for example, would use the information on an application form for a bank account for different purposes. The name and address might be checked with a credit agency to see if the person is in debt or not, the person's employer details would be checked out, the person's mother's maiden name would be used to confirm identity and so on. The information would then be entered in a computer so that a record of the person's new account could be established.

◆ Explain that sometimes information is used to write up a report, for example consumer surveys. Provide an example of a completed form similar to the one presented in Activity sheet 1. Tell them that you will show them how to write a report using the information from this form.

◆ Explain that reports are written to provide a summary of the information or to present the most important or most relevant information.

◆ Model how to write the information contained in the form in sentences. Ask the children to suggest how to begin the report and the kinds of words and phrases to use. What information is vital? What information is not so important?

◆ Tell the children that they will now have a go at writing a report themselves. Explain the three different activities and tell the children that they will be sharing their reports with others at the end of the lesson.

◆ Using the differentiated activity sheets

Activity sheet 1

This activity sheet is aimed at those children who need support in writing a report. The task is presented as a cloze activity where the children are required to use the information provided to complete the sentences. The teacher may need to work with this group to help the children read the form.

Activity sheet 2

This activity is for children who are more confident readers and writers. They are required to make a decision based on evidence in the forms. Explain that there is no 'right' answer. All they need to remember is to make sure they back up their decision with reasons.

Activity sheet 3

This activity is for more able children because it requires them to synthesize information from six different forms. They are required to calculate the ages of the people by using the date of births. Tell them to make a summary of all the information for their report, using the answers to the questions as well as any other information they think is important.

◆ Plenary session

Bring the whole class together again to share their work. Ask someone from each group to remind others what their activity entailed and then ask several people to read out their reports. Are the reports clear and easy to understand? Has all the relevant information been included? What reasons were given for the best person for the job in Activity 2? Do others agree? Could any other questions be included on any of the forms to provide extra/more relevant information?

Official forms

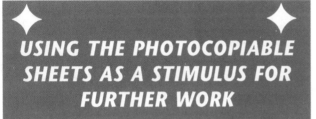

USING THE PHOTOCOPIABLE SHEETS AS A STIMULUS FOR FURTHER WORK

✦ Ask the children using Activity sheet 1 to write a formal letter to Miss Browne, asking her to attend an interview for an engineering firm.

✦ Ask the children using Activity sheet 2 to work out a list of questions they would ask the applicants at a job interview. Act out the interviews!

✦ Ask the children using Activity sheet 3 to design a more detailed questionnaire sheet about shopping in their local area. Send the sheet home for parents to complete in order to carry out a 'real' survey.

✦ Find out more information about the jobs mentioned on the sheets. Ask a shop manager, market researcher and an engineer to give a talk to the class.

✦ Do a class survey to find out the types of jobs the children would like to do. Ask them to write a paragraph giving their reasons why. Use the information to make a class display about jobs.

✦ Use a thesaurus to find out other words for words on the forms. How many different words could be used for 'occupation', for example?

OTHER IDEAS FOR USING OFFICIAL FORMS

✦ Make a collection of official language used on forms. Make a glossary or dictionary to explain the meaning of the terms.

✦ Investigate any information notes and guidance that are provided with forms. How much 'gobbledegook' is there? What's the longest, most involved sentence?

✦ Ask the children to design their own form for children new to the class to complete. What information would they like to know about them?

✦ Make a class application form for a real or invented job(s) in the school or class, such as a new club. Write letters to the applicants and ask them to write back their responses. Have interviews for the jobs. Make up notices announcing the results.

✦ Complete passport applications. Ask the children to design and make their own passports using the information. Use the passports to 'visit' places around the world by using reference books to find out information about the places.

✦ Look at other examples of official language in public notices, legal documents and so on. Write letters in response to them. Investigate language used in them which is not usually part of everyday speech, for example, 'hereto', 'contemporaneous with', 'hereby', 'in respect thereof'.

✦ Miss Browne's application ✦

✦ Use the information contained in Miss Jennifer Browne's application form
  to complete the report about her.

Title: Miss ✔   Mrs ☐   Ms ☐
     Master ☐   Mr ☐   Other ☐

First names: JENNIFER MARY
Last name: BROWNE
Maiden name: N/A

Date of birth: | 0 | 5 | 1 | 0 | 8 | 0 |
Postal address: 24 TOWNLEY AVE
MARYWEATHER, OXON
Postcode: | O | X | 1 | 2 | 4 | M | W |
Telephone: 01334 234567
Marital status: SINGLE
Number of dependants: NONE
Do you own your own home? NO
Current occupation: STUDENT
Employer's name and address:
OXFORD EDUCATION AUTHORITY
COUNTY HALL, OXFORD
Nature of employer's business:
EDUCATION

Please list your hobbies: READING,
SWIMMING, COOKING, SKY-DIVING
Do you have a driver's licence? YES

Are you interested in full or part time employment?
FULL TIME

Qualifications: A LEVEL MATHS, ENGLISH
AND FRENCH

Please tick the kind of employment you are looking
for:

building trade ☐	finance ☐
advertising ☐	education ☐
retail ☐	hotel ☐
transport ☐	manufacturing ☐
legal ☐	catering ☐
medical ☐	engineering ✔
post office ☐	fashion ☐
services ☐	armed forces ☐

other (please state): _____

✦ Use this information to complete the report below:

Miss Jennifer Browne lives at _____.

She is _____years old. Currently she is a student and is employed by

_____.

Miss Browne's hobbies are _____.

She has a driver's licence and is interested in _____ work. She has the

following qualifications:_____. She is

looking for work of the following kind: _____.

Using non-fiction

Developing
Literacy
Skills

Photocopiable

KS2 Y5–6/P6–7

©Hopscotch Educational Publishing

55

◆ Make your choice ◆

◆ Here is an advertisement for a job. Two people have applied for it. Read their application forms below and decide which person you think best suits the job.

> **Wanted: Shop Manager**. Must be aged between 25–35 and have clean driver's licence. Experience in retailing essential. Interest in fashion and bookkeeping an advantage. Required to use computers and work with lots of different people.

Title: **Mr**   First names: **Mark Phillip**

Last name: **Boyer**

Date of birth: **25/03/70**

Address: **14 Downend St, Templeton, TT2 5DN**

Current employment: **Shop assistant in men's fashion department**

Qualifications: **GCSE Maths, English, Computer studies**

Hobbies/interests: **skiing, fishing, football, travel**

Do you have a driver's licence? **No, but I'm keen to get one.**

Other information: **I am honest and trustworthy. I work hard and want to be part of a team.**

Title: **Miss** First names: **Sonia Maria**

Last name: **Lever**

Date of birth: **02/07/65**

Address: **18 Speedwell St, Oakville OK6 4SP**

Current employment: **Shop assistant in furniture department**

Qualifications: **GCSE Maths, Art and design**

Hobbies/interests: **fashion designing, reading, meeting people**

Do you have a driver's licence? **Yes**

Other information: **I am very ambitious and keen to learn new things. I am interested in fashion and like to work with people.**

◆ Write down in sentences all your reasons for selecting this person. Make your report good enough to convince the boss who is best!

I think _____ is the best person for this job because

✦ Market research ✦

✦ A market researcher recently asked six people to complete a form about their shopping habits. Read through each form and then answer the questions.

Name: Daniel Myers
DOB: 24.2.80
Car owner? Yes
What transport do you use for shopping?
    car ✔
    public transport ☐
What do you usually buy?
music ✔   books ☐
food ☐   computer items ☐
clothes ✔   household goods ☐
jewellery ☐   toys, games ☐
Pet hate about shopping:
queues

Name: Susan Shaw
DOB: 15.12.75
Car owner? Yes
What transport do you use for shopping?
    car ✔
    public transport ☐
What do you usually buy?
music ☐   books ✔
food ☐   computer items ☐
clothes ✔   household goods ☐
jewellery ☐   toys, games ☐
Pet hate about shopping:
hot shops

Name: Sarah Ahmed
DOB: 13.7.81
Car owner? No
What transport do you use for shopping?
    car ☐
    public transport ✔
What do you usually buy?
music ✔   books ☐
food ✔   computer items ☐
clothes ✔   household goods ☐
jewellery ☐   toys, games ☐
Pet hate about shopping:
Not having enough money

Name: Maria Antonelli
DOB: 4.9.76
Car owner? No
What transport do you use for shopping?
    car ☐
    public transport ✔
What do you usually buy?
music ✔   books ☐
food ☐   computer items ☐
clothes ✔   household goods ☐
jewellery ☐   toys, games ☐
Pet hate about shopping:
queues

Name: Michael Young
DOB: 4.11.77
Car owner? Yes
What transport do you use for shopping?
    car ✔
    public transport ☐
What do you usually buy?
music ✔   books ☐
food ☐   computer items ✔
clothes ✔   household goods ☐
jewellery ☐   toys, games ☐
Pet hate about shopping:
crowded shops

Name: Michelle Peters
DOB: 30.12.74
Car owner? Yes
What transport do you use for shopping?
    car ✔
    public transport ☐
What do you usually buy?
music ☐   books ☐
food ☐   computer items ☐
clothes ✔   household goods ☐
jewellery ☐   toys, games ☐
Pet hate about shopping:
queues

---

1 Were the people mainly male or female? _____

2 What age range were they between? _____

3 What things do they buy most? _____

4 What do most of them dislike about shopping? _____

✦ On the back of this sheet, write a report about the research. Write your report in sentences.

Encyclopedias

 Overall aims

- To practise locating information using encyclopedias.
- To write notes and summaries derived from reading.
- To use flow diagrams to make a summary of information.

 Suggested texts

A range of different encyclopedias.

 **LESSON ONE**

 Intended learning

- To practise locating information efficiently using encyclopedias.
- To write notes and summaries derived from reading.

 Starting point: Whole class

- If appropriate, visit the school library to revise location and types of encyclopedias in the school. Discuss the purpose of encyclopedias. Talk about how the volumes of the encyclopedias are organised, such as numerical, alphabetical, chronological and so on. Look at the general layout of the books inside to note how the pages are set out and numbered. Are headers used in the same way as in dictionaries?
- Discuss how to use the index volumes of the encyclopedias to look up subjects. Discuss the meaning of the numbers and/or letters next to the entries in the index and then use these to find the correct volume and page.
- Ask the children to remind you how to skim and scan a page in order to find the section required. Remind them to refer also to any diagrams or pictures which might relate to the entry.
- Once the correct section has been located, discuss how to go about finding the details required. Remind them how useful it is to have some paper

ready to make some notes as they read the information. What can they do if they come across words they do not understand? Talk about using the surrounding text, dictionaries, glossaries and cross-referencing with other encyclopedias and information books to help them.

 Group activities

- To practise finding the correct volume for specific topics, ask the children to use the information on the spines and/or the index volumes to write down the volumes to match a list of prepared topic headings.
- Photocopy a page from an index volume and make up a crossword puzzle or quiz using information from this page.
- Photocopy a page from an encyclopedia and ask the children to underline the key words and phrases to make a summary of the information.
- Read out some information from an encyclopedia to the children. Ask them to draw a picture, write a paragraph or label a diagram which summarises the information. This provides practise in putting things 'in your own words' and encourages the children not to copy from the text.

 Plenary session

Bring the whole class together again to share the activities. Check the answers to the first two activities and then ask some children to read out their summary of information from the third activity. Do others agree that the main points/ideas have been included in the summary? Compare the paragraphs/drawings/illustrations for the last activity. How similar are they? Was specialist knowledge needed to do the diagram? How could you find out more information? Discuss using encyclopedias in general. What problems do the children have when using them? How can these problems be overcome?

◆ LESSON TWO ◆

◆ Intended learning

◆ To use flow diagrams to make a summary of information.

◆ Starting point: Whole class

◆ Ask the children to tell you ways to make a summary of information from encyclopedias – notes, underlining main ideas, doing a diagram or drawing, listing key words and so on.
◆ Explain that a very good way of summarising information that is made up of lots of steps in a process is to do a flow diagram.
◆ Demonstrate a flow diagram using an enlarged copy of a recipe. List the steps in the recipe. Then model how to write the steps in order with arrows joining up each stage, for example:

Pizza

take wrapping off prepared pizza base
↓
strain tin of tomatoes
↓
put tomatoes in bowl
↓
add pinch salt, pepper and sugar
↓
spread tomato mixture over pizza base
↓
add chopped cheese, onion and green peppers
↓
sprinkle small amount of dried herbs
↓
put pizza on baking tray
↓
bake in hot oven for 30 minutes

◆ Explain that the diagram can be set out down the page as above or they can be drawn across the page. Tell them that sometimes the diagram can include illustrations as well. The important thing to remember, however, is that all the main steps are included, in the correct order.

◆ Tell the children that they will now have the opportunity to write their own flow diagram about the process of minting or coin making. Explain that each group will be finding out about a different stage in the minting process and that they will share their information with the whole class in order to find out about all three stages.

Using the differentiated activity sheets

Activity sheet 1

This activity sheet is aimed at those children who will need support with setting out a flow diagram. The text is simple and the process described is easy to understand.

Activity sheet 2

This activity is aimed at those children who are capable of setting out a flow diagram themselves. The children in this group could work in pairs to help each other understand the process involved and how to set out the diagram.

Activity sheet 3

This activity is for more able children. They have to decide which information is relevant to the task before they can begin the flow diagram.

◆ Plenary session

Bring the whole class together again when the activities are complete. Ask someone from each group to explain the steps in their stage of the coin-making process in order to understand the entire process from beginning to end. Share the flow diagrams. Are they clear and correctly sequenced? Do the diagrams help to summarise the information well? Explain that this method is a good way to record and remember the stages in even complicated processes and is another good example of a way to summarise information.

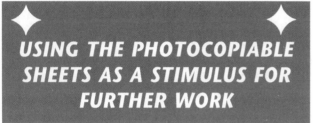

Encyclopedias

◆ USING THE PHOTOCOPIABLE SHEETS AS A STIMULUS FOR FURTHER WORK ◆

◆ Make a whole-class wall mural of a large illustrated flow diagram of the stages in making coins. Use reference books to find out what the parts, tools and machines look like.

◆ Write letters to the Royal Mint (Llantrisant, Pontyclun, Mid Glam. CF7 8YT) to find out more about British coins.

◆ Use encyclopedias to find out information about the history of coins.

◆ Design a new coin collection for Britain. Write an advertising campaign to promote it.

◆ Find out about metals and alloys. Relate to work in science on magnetism.

◆ Discuss other diagrammatical forms of presenting information, such as hierarchies, plans, maps, cross-sections, time-lines and cycles. Relate to work in other subject areas, such as history, geography and science.

◆ Make flow diagrams of other processes, such as making a cup of tea.

◆ OTHER IDEAS FOR USING ENCYCLOPEDIAS ◆

◆ Make quiz or question cards which relate to specific encyclopedia sets in the school. Allow time in each library lesson to complete a card.

◆ Challenge older children to make an encyclopedia for younger children that relates to their class topics.

◆ Compare CD-ROM encyclopedias with book format. Which is easier to use? Why? What are the similarities and differences? What are the advantages and disadvantages of each type?

◆ Discuss differences between information books and encyclopedias. How easy are they to keep up to date? Look at year volumes – what new information has been added? Country boundaries, for example.

◆ Compare entries from very old encyclopedias to new ones. Do 'facts' change over time? Why?

◆ Ask the children to make up crossword puzzles where the clues relate to specific volumes or pages in a volume.

◆ When researching a particular topic, read the information from the encyclopedia onto a tape to make the encyclopedia more accessible to less able readers.

◆ Ask the children to write a glossary of terms which relate to a specific section of an encyclopedia. Display the glossary to help others understand the technical language used in the passage.

Developing
literacy
Skills

◆ Making coins ◆

✦ The information below outlines the final stage in making coins. Use a dictionary to look up the meaning of the underlined words. Then use the information to complete the flow diagram at the bottom of the page.

> The final stage of making coins is when the coin-sized discs or blanks of metal are made into a finished coin.
>
> First, the blanks are fed into a coin press by a <u>hopper</u>. The press strikes the <u>obverse</u> and <u>reverse</u> sides of the coin as well as doing the edging if necessary.
>
> The press squeezes the blank between the two dies (the coin design) using a pressure of up to 150 tonnes. In this way, the blank has both sides of the coin pressed into it at the same time. This process is called striking.
>
> After striking, the coins are ejected from the press and fall into a container. The coins are then inspected carefully.
>
> After inspection the coins are counted into bags using a telling machine. The bags are picked up by a robotic arm and placed onto pallets where they are wrapped in plastic. Labels are then put on to show the type and number of coins in the bag. They are then transferred to a storage place before being despatched.

✦ Complete this flow diagram. Remember to write the stages in the correct order. Use the correct words to name the stages and machinery used.

blanks → hopper → _____ → container ↓

　　　　　　　　blank is squeezed between
　　　　　　　　two _____
　　　　　　　　this is called _____

　　　　　　　　　　　　　　　　　　　　　　_____

　　　　　　　　　　　　　　　　　　　　　　　　↙

　　　　　　　　　　　　　　　　　counted into
　　　　　　　　　　　　　　　　　_____

wrapped ← _____ ← telling machine

↓

_____ → stored → _____

Using non-fiction
KS2: Y5–6/P6–7

Developing
Literacy
Skills

Photocopiable
©Hopscotch Educational Publishing

61

✦ Making coins ✦

✦ You are going to write a flow diagram for the second stage of coin making – the manufacture of blanks. Read the inform tion below very carefully. Use a dictionary to look up the meaning of any words you do not know. Then underline each stage of the blank-making process.

Raw materials such as copper, nickel, zinc and tin are made up into 'furnace charges' containing the correct amounts of each material to make the alloy needed. For example, £1 coins are made up of 70% copper, 5.5% nickel and 24.5% zinc. The charges are melted in furnaces at temperatures over 1000 degrees celsius.

The molten metal produced is then poured into a holding and casting furnace. This furnace shapes and moulds the metal into a continuous slab about 15mm thick. Saws cut the slabs into bars of metal, 10 metres long. These bars each weigh 250kg.

Next the bars are put into a tandem rolling mill. This mill reduces the thickness of the bars to 3mm and then changes the bars into coils.

After passing through the tandem rolling mill, a number of coils are welded together to make one big coil. This coil goes to the finishing mill. This mill makes the metal into the correct thickness for the type of coin.

The coil goes to a blanking press. This press makes coin-sized discs called blanks. The blanks are cut out. Finally, the blanks go into a pickling machine where they are cleaned.

✦ Use the underlined text to draw and label your flow diagram here. Make sure you have the stages in the correct order. Use the correct names of each stage and type of machinery.

◆ Making coins ◆

◆ You are going to write a flow diagram for the first stage of coin making – making the dies. Read the information below, using a dictionary to look up the meaning of any words you do not know. Decide which parts of this information refer to die making then use these facts to write your flow diagram.

Minting of coins began in Britain in the early part of the first century. Some of these early coins were cast in moulds but later on they were struck by hand. Roman coins were used in Britain when the Romans lived here and some of these were made at a mint in London. By about 1279, the mint was located in the Tower of London and remained there for over 500 years. Mills and presses were introduced in the seventeenth century. The mint moved to Little Tower Hill in 1811 where it remained until 1968 when a new factory was opened in Llantrisant, near Cardiff. Minting is still carried out there today.

The production of the coins involves three separate processes – the engraving of dies, the manufacture of blanks and the striking of the blanks to transform them into coins.

Die-making begins with a designer who designs the coins. An artist then makes a plaster model of the obverse and reverse designs of the coin. This model is large (30cm in diameter) and circular. The model is used to make a rubber mould which is then electroplated with nickel and copper. This makes a metal reproduction of the model, called an electrotype.

The electrotype is put onto a reducing machine where its design is scanned by a tracer. The tracer transmits the details of the design to a cutting tool. The design is reduced to the size of the actual coin and the cutting tool copies the design into a block of steel. This becomes the master punch.

The master punch is used to make a matrix which is called the master die. The dies are used to 'stamp' both sides of the coin in the third process of coin making – striking the blanks.

◆ Draw and label your flow diagram here:

✦ Book review – non-fiction ✦

✦ Title: _____

✦ Author: _____

✦ Publisher: _____

✦ Illustrator: _____

✦ Write a brief summary of what the book contains.

✦ What age group do you think this book is suitable for? Give your reasons.

✦ Give your opinion about the following things:

   a) the use of diagrams and illustrations

   b) the amount of information provided

   c) how easy it is to find what you want in the book

✦ Would you recommend this book to others? Say why or why not.

Continue on the back of this sheet

Photocopiable

©Hopscotch Educational Publishing